The

Galaxy S25

Guide for Beginners

A Simple and Easy to Follow Guide to Set
Up and Use Your New Phone Like a Pro

Colleen Dutton

Disclaimer

This book is intended solely for educational purposes. It provides readers with step-by-step instructions and guidance to navigate and use the Samsung Galaxy S25. The information in this book is based on publicly available knowledge at the time of publication. The author, Colleen Dutton, and the publisher are not affiliated with Samsung Electronics, nor is this book endorsed by or sponsored by the company.

The content in this book is not intended to promote or sell any products or services, nor does it serve as a commercial advertisement for any specific brand. It is strictly an educational resource to help users maximize their experience with the Samsung Galaxy S25.

Every effort has been made to ensure the accuracy of the information presented in this book; however, the author and publisher cannot be held liable for any errors, omissions, or changes in the technology or device features after publication.

By reading this book, you acknowledge and agree that the use of the Samsung Galaxy S25 is at your own risk, and the author and publisher will not be held responsible for any issues or damages arising from the use of the content provided.

Table of Contents

Introduction

The Samsung Galaxy S25 is one of the newest and most exciting smartphones released by Samsung. With powerful features and sleek design, it offers an incredible experience for users who love modern technology. Whether you are a first-time smartphone user or upgrading to a new phone, the Galaxy S25 makes it easy to enjoy all of its features right from the start.

Samsung has always been known for producing high-quality smartphones, and the Galaxy S25 is no different. This phone is designed to help you do everything you need—whether that's staying connected with friends and family, taking amazing pictures, watching videos, or getting things done for work or school. It has a stunning display, a long-lasting battery, a powerful camera, and much more to make your life easier and more fun.

The Galaxy S25 is part of Samsung's Galaxy S series, which is known for its top-of-the-line features. With each new phone in the series, Samsung adds new and improved technologies, and the Galaxy S25 is no exception. One of the highlights of the Galaxy S25 is its powerful processor. This makes the phone fast and smooth when using apps, playing games, or browsing the web. Whether you're running several apps at once or simply scrolling through social media, the Galaxy S25 can handle it all without any lag.

Another great feature of the Galaxy S25 is its camera. The phone comes with multiple lenses, allowing you to take beautiful photos and videos in any situation. Whether you're capturing a scenic view, snapping a selfie, or taking a group picture, the camera's advanced settings will make sure every shot looks fantastic. Even in low-light conditions, the Galaxy S25's camera performs well, meaning you don't have to worry about poor quality photos when it's dark out.

Battery life is also a major concern for smartphone users, but the Galaxy S25 has a long-lasting battery to keep you going all day. Whether you're streaming videos, chatting with friends, or browsing the internet, you won't have to worry about your phone running out of battery too soon. Plus, it supports fast charging, so you can quickly power up your phone when you need to.

The Galaxy S25 also has a smooth and clear display. Whether you're watching videos, playing games, or reading, the display is vibrant and easy on the eyes. The phone's design is slim and modern, making it comfortable to hold and easy to use with one hand. It also has features like face recognition and fingerprint scanning to help keep your phone secure.

Samsung has also made it easier to use the Galaxy S25 with their software, One UI, which helps you easily navigate the phone and customize it to fit your needs. From the home screen to apps and settings, everything is organized in a simple and intuitive way, making it easy for anyone to use.

The Samsung Galaxy S25 is a fantastic phone for anyone looking for an easy-to-use device with powerful features. Whether you're using it for personal or professional tasks, this phone offers everything you need in one sleek package. From its fast performance to its stunning camera, the Galaxy S25 is a device that can make your day-to-day life more enjoyable and efficient.

Chapter 1: Getting Started

Unboxing Your Phone

When you first open the box of your Samsung Galaxy S25, you'll be greeted with the phone itself, neatly packaged to ensure it stays safe during transport. Unboxing your new device can be an exciting experience, and it's important to take your time to make sure you have all the necessary accessories and information to get started.

Inside the box, you'll typically find the following items:

- Samsung Galaxy S25 phone: The main device that you'll be using.
- USB-C cable: This is used for charging the phone and connecting it to other devices. Samsung has moved to USB-C for faster data transfer and charging speeds.
- Wall charger: While some versions of the phone may not include this, a wall charger will

generally be included for quick charging. The Galaxy S25 supports fast charging, so you'll want to use the charger provided for the best results.

- SIM card ejector tool: This small tool helps you insert or remove the SIM card tray from your phone.
- User manual and warranty information: These papers explain how to use your phone and cover any warranty details or return policies.

Once you have removed all the items from the box, take a moment to inspect your new phone. You will notice the shiny and sleek design, the display with minimal bezels, and the premium build quality. Your Galaxy S25 might come with a plastic film covering the screen for protection, which you can easily peel off. There may also be a protective cover on the back of the phone.

It's a good idea to keep the packaging in case you need to return the phone or store accessories safely later. The box is also useful for keeping your phone's receipts, warranty information, and other documentation.

Inserting the SIM Card

Before you can start using your Galaxy S25, you'll need to insert your SIM card, which allows your phone to connect to your mobile network. If you're upgrading from an older phone, your current SIM card might work with the Galaxy S25, but if you're switching from a different carrier or starting with a new service, you might need to get a new SIM card from your carrier.

Here's how to insert the SIM card:

1. Locate the SIM card tray: On the Galaxy S25, the SIM card tray is usually located on the left-hand side of the phone. It's a small, rectangular slot near the top edge of the phone. There will be a small pinhole next to the tray.

2. Use the SIM card ejector tool: Insert the ejector tool into the tiny hole next to the SIM tray. Press gently until the tray pops out. You don't need to apply much force.

3. Place your SIM card: Carefully place your SIM card into the tray. Make sure the metal contacts on the SIM card are facing down. The tray is designed to only fit the SIM card in one direction, so there's no need to worry about aligning it wrong.

4. Insert the tray back into the phone: Once the SIM card is in place, gently slide the tray back into the phone's slot. Ensure that it is completely closed to prevent the tray from being exposed.

Once the SIM card is inserted, your phone should automatically detect it, and you'll see the signal strength indicator in the top right corner of the screen. If the phone doesn't recognize the SIM card, you might need to restart the phone or check if the card is inserted correctly.

Turning On and Setting Up Your Phone

Now that your SIM card is in place, you're ready to turn on your Samsung Galaxy S25 and begin setting it up. The power button is located on the right side of the phone. Press and hold the power button for a few seconds until the Samsung logo appears on the screen. The phone will start booting up, which may take a few moments.

Once the phone turns on, you'll be prompted to begin the setup process. Follow these steps to get your phone up and running:

1. Language Selection: The first screen will ask you to choose your preferred language. Select your language from the list, and press "Next."

2. Connect to Wi-Fi: The next screen will prompt you to connect to a Wi-Fi network. Choose your home Wi-Fi network from the list, and enter the Wi-Fi password. If

you don't want to connect to Wi-Fi right now, you can skip this step, but it's recommended to connect to Wi-Fi to save on mobile data and allow software updates to download.

3. Agree to Terms and Conditions: You'll be asked to accept the terms and conditions for using your Samsung Galaxy S25. It's a good idea to read through them, but you can click "Agree" to move forward.

4. Data Transfer Options: If you're upgrading from an old phone, you'll have the option to transfer your data to your new Galaxy S25. You can use Samsung's Smart Switch app, which allows you to transfer contacts, photos, messages, and apps from your old device wirelessly or using a cable.

5. Set Up Security: You'll be asked to set up a method for securing your phone. You can choose from options such as a PIN, password, pattern lock, or biometric security (fingerprint or face recognition). Setting up

security is important to protect your personal information and keep your phone secure.

6. Software Updates: After the initial setup, your phone may prompt you to check for software updates. It's always a good idea to install the latest updates to ensure your phone runs smoothly and securely.

Once you've completed the setup, your Galaxy S25 is ready to be used!

Signing In to Your Google and Samsung Accounts

To get the most out of your Galaxy S25, it's important to sign in to both your Google and Samsung accounts. These accounts will allow you to access a range of services, including apps, cloud storage, and settings synchronization.

1. Signing In to Google Account:

After your phone finishes setting up, you'll be asked to sign in to your Google account. If you already have a Gmail account, simply enter your email and password. If you don't have one, you can create a new account. Signing in to your Google account will give you access to:

- Google Play Store for downloading apps
- Google Photos for cloud storage of photos and videos
- Google Drive for storing documents and files
- Gmail for email
- Google Calendar for syncing your events and reminders

Once signed in, your phone will automatically sync all your Google services, making it easy to access your emails, files, and other data across devices.

2. Signing In to Samsung Account:

After setting up your Google account, you'll also be asked to sign in to your Samsung account. If you don't have one, you can create it for free. A Samsung account will provide access to:

- Samsung Cloud for backing up data and syncing content across Samsung devices
- Samsung Galaxy Store for downloading exclusive apps
- Samsung Pay for making payments using your phone
- Access to Samsung's customer support services and warranty registration

Signing in to your Samsung account is optional, but it's highly recommended for taking full advantage of the Galaxy S25's features.

Once both accounts are set up, you're ready to explore everything your Galaxy S25 has to offer.

Chapter 2: Navigating Your Phone

Understanding the Home Screen

The home screen on your Samsung Galaxy S25 is the main starting point when you use your phone. It's the first screen you see when you unlock your phone, and it holds all your important apps, widgets, and shortcuts. Understanding the home screen layout is crucial for navigating your phone smoothly and efficiently. Let's go over the basic elements that make up the home screen on your Galaxy S25.

1. The Status Bar

At the top of the home screen, you'll see the status bar. This is where your phone shows important information about your device. The status bar displays:

- Battery level: A small icon that shows how much battery is remaining.

- Signal strength: An icon that shows how strong your mobile network signal is.

- Wi-Fi: If you're connected to a Wi-Fi network, the Wi-Fi symbol will appear here.

- Notifications: Any alerts or notifications, such as text messages, app updates, or reminders, will appear here. You can swipe down from the status bar to see more details.

2. The Home Screen

The home screen is where you place your most-used apps and widgets. You can have multiple home screens on your Galaxy S25. Each screen can be customized to display the apps or widgets that matter most to you.

- Apps: Apps are represented by icons on your home screen. These can be apps you use every day, such as your messaging app, camera, or social media apps.

- Widgets: Widgets are small, interactive elements that provide information or shortcuts to specific features. For example, you might have a weather widget that shows the current temperature or a calendar widget that shows your next appointment.

You can swipe left or right on the home screen to move between different screens. If you want to add or remove screens, you can do that in the settings as well.

3. The Dock

At the bottom of the home screen, you'll find the dock. This is a fixed area where you can place your most frequently used apps. No matter which home screen you're on, the apps in the dock will always be visible. You can place four apps in the dock, such as Phone, Messages, Internet, and Camera, for quick access.

4. The App Icons

Every app you download will have an icon that appears on the home screen. Tap on an icon to open that app. You can move these icons around or group them together into folders to make it easier to access your favorite apps.

The home screen on your Galaxy S25 acts as a control center, where you can easily access apps and stay informed with notifications and widgets. Understanding how to navigate the home screen is the first step in using your phone efficiently.

Using the App Drawer

The app drawer is where all your installed apps are stored. It's separate from the home screen, allowing you to keep your home screen organized while still having quick access to any app you've installed.

Here's how to access and use the app drawer:

1. Opening the App Drawer

To open the app drawer, swipe up from the bottom of the screen. This action will bring up a list of all the apps installed on your device. The apps are displayed in alphabetical order by default, but you can change the sorting method in the settings.

2. Searching for Apps

If you have a lot of apps installed, finding the one you need can take time. To search for an app, simply tap on the search bar at the top of the app drawer. Start typing the name of the app, and the phone will show suggestions as you type. You can then tap on the app you want to open.

3. Organizing Your Apps

In the app drawer, you can organize your apps in different ways:

- Create folders: You can group similar apps into folders, such as a folder for all social media apps or a folder for your work apps. To create a folder, press and hold an app icon, then drag it on top of another app. A folder will automatically be created, and you can add more apps to it.

- Rearrange apps: To rearrange the apps in the app drawer, press and hold an app icon, then drag it to a new location in the list.

4. Accessing App Settings

Each app may have its own settings that you can adjust. To access these settings, press and hold the app icon in the app drawer and tap on "App Info." From there, you can change settings like notifications, permissions, and storage.

5. Removing Apps from the App Drawer

If you no longer need an app, you can easily uninstall it from the app drawer. Press and hold the app icon, then tap on "Uninstall" or "Remove." Confirm that you want to remove the app, and it will be deleted from your phone.

The app drawer is an essential part of your Galaxy S25 experience, giving you access to all your apps in one convenient place. It helps keep your home screen clean and organized while still allowing you to easily find and open apps.

Customizing Your Home Screen

One of the best things about your Galaxy S25 is how customizable it is. You can adjust the home screen to reflect your personal style and make it as efficient as possible. Here are some simple ways you can customize your home screen:

1. Changing Wallpaper

Your wallpaper is the background image of your home screen. Changing it allows you to personalize the look of your phone. To change your wallpaper:

- Press and hold an empty space on your home screen.
- Tap "Wallpapers" from the options that appear.
- You can choose from a set of pre-installed wallpapers or select one of your own photos. After choosing your desired wallpaper, tap "Set Wallpaper" to apply it.

2. Adding and Removing Widgets

Widgets are small tools that show information or provide quick access to features like the weather, calendar, or news updates. You can add widgets to your home screen to make it more functional.

To add a widget:

- Press and hold an empty space on your home screen.
- Tap "Widgets" from the options that appear.
- Browse through the available widgets and select one you want to add.
- Drag the widget to your home screen and position it where you want it.

To remove a widget, press and hold it, then drag it to the "Remove" section at the top of the screen.

3. Organizing Apps into Folders

As mentioned earlier, you can organize apps into folders on your home screen. This is useful if you have many apps and want to keep everything tidy. To create a folder:

- Press and hold an app icon.

- Drag it on top of another app you want to group it with.
- The folder will be created, and you can rename it to something that makes sense, like "Games" or "Work."

4. Changing the Layout

You can adjust the grid layout of your home screen to fit more or fewer apps. To change the layout:

- Press and hold an empty space on your home screen.
- Tap "Home screen settings."
- Under "Grid," you can choose how many apps you want to show in each row and column. You can select between different grid sizes to suit your needs.

5. Moving and Removing Apps

To move an app on your home screen, press and hold the app icon, then drag it to a new location. If you no longer want an app on the home screen but don't want to uninstall it, you can remove it from the screen by dragging it to the "Remove" section at the top. This will not uninstall the app; it will just remove the shortcut from the home screen.

6. Changing the Icon Shape

Samsung allows you to change the shape of your app icons to give your phone a more customized look. To do this:

- Open the "Home screen settings."
- Look for the option to "Icon Shape" and select your preferred style, such as rounded or square.

By customizing your home screen, you can make your Galaxy S25 truly your own. Whether you prefer a clean and minimalistic layout or a vibrant, widget-filled screen, the Galaxy S25 offers many options to personalize your phone and make it work for you.

Navigating your Galaxy S25's home screen, app drawer, and customization options is key to making your experience seamless and enjoyable. With just a few simple steps, you can set up your phone exactly the way you want it and enjoy a personalized, user-friendly device.

Chapter 3: Setting Up Basic Features

Connecting to Wi-Fi

One of the first things you'll need to do when setting up your Samsung Galaxy S25 is to connect it to Wi-Fi. A stable Wi-Fi connection allows you to browse the internet, download apps, and stay connected with friends and family without using your mobile data. Fortunately, connecting your phone to Wi-Fi is simple and quick. Here's how you can do it:

Step 1: Open the Settings App

The easiest way to begin the Wi-Fi connection process is by opening the Settings app on your phone. You can do this by swiping down from the top of the screen to access the notification panel, and then tapping the gear icon. Alternatively, you can find the Settings app in the App Drawer.

Step 2: Navigate to Connections

Once you're in the Settings menu, look for the "Connections" section. This is where you can manage all network-related settings, including Wi-Fi, mobile data, and Bluetooth. Tap on "Connections," and then tap "Wi-Fi" to open the Wi-Fi settings.

Step 3: Turn on Wi-Fi

If Wi-Fi is not already turned on, you'll need to toggle the switch to turn it on. Once enabled, your phone will automatically search for available networks in the vicinity.

Step 4: Select a Network

Once your phone has scanned for available Wi-Fi networks, a list of networks will appear on the screen. You will see the names (SSID) of Wi-Fi networks nearby. Choose the Wi-Fi network you want to connect to by tapping on its name.

Step 5: Enter the Password

If the network you selected is password-protected, a prompt will appear asking you to enter the Wi-Fi password. Type in the password exactly as it's provided—Wi-Fi passwords are case-sensitive. Once you've entered the password, tap "Connect."

Step 6: Confirm Connection

After your phone successfully connects to the Wi-Fi network, you should see a Wi-Fi symbol appear in the status bar at the top of the screen. This confirms that you're connected and can now browse the internet or use online services.

If you ever need to disconnect from the network, simply tap "Disconnect" in the Wi-Fi settings or toggle off the Wi-Fi switch.

Troubleshooting Wi-Fi Connections

In rare cases, you might experience issues connecting to a Wi-Fi network. If you're having trouble:

- Make sure you're within range of the Wi-Fi router.

- Ensure you've entered the correct password.

- Try restarting your phone or the router to refresh the connection.

- If the issue persists, check your phone's software settings or consult your internet service provider.

Connecting to Wi-Fi is a fundamental feature that enables your Samsung Galaxy S25 to function effectively in a connected world.

Setting Up Fingerprint or Face Recognition

Your Samsung Galaxy S25 is equipped with biometric security features like fingerprint recognition and face recognition, both of which allow you to unlock your phone and access apps more securely. Setting up these features ensures that only you can access your device, adding a layer of protection. Here's how to set them up:

Fingerprint Recognition

Step 1: Open the Settings App

As with most settings on your Galaxy S25, the first step is to open the Settings app. Tap the gear icon from the notification panel or the App Drawer.

Step 2: Navigate to Biometrics and Security

In the Settings menu, find and tap on "Biometrics and Security." This is where you will find all security-related options for your phone, including fingerprint, face recognition, and screen lock.

Step 3: Tap Fingerprints

Under "Biometrics and Security," tap "Fingerprints." This option will allow you to register your fingerprint for unlocking your phone.

Step 4: Register Your Fingerprint

Tap "Add fingerprint" to begin the registration process. The phone will ask you to place your finger on the fingerprint sensor located under the display of your Galaxy S25. Gently place your finger on the sensor and lift it off. The phone will ask you to repeat this several times to ensure it captures a complete scan of your fingerprint.

Step 5: Set a Backup Lock

You will be asked to set a backup lock method, such as a PIN, password, or pattern. This backup lock will be used in case the fingerprint sensor fails to recognize your fingerprint.

Step 6: Complete the Setup

Once your fingerprint is successfully registered, you'll be able to use it to unlock your phone, sign into apps, and authorize payments.

Face Recognition

Step 1: Access Biometrics and Security

As with fingerprint recognition, open the Settings app, then tap on "Biometrics and Security" to access the security features.

Step 2: Tap Face Recognition

Find and tap "Face Recognition" under the Biometrics section. The phone will guide you through the setup process.

Step 3: Register Your Face

Tap "Register" to begin the process of registering your face. You will need to hold the phone at eye level in a well-lit area. The phone will ask you to align your face within the frame on the screen. It may ask you to move your head slightly to help capture your face from different angles. Make sure your face is well-lit for better accuracy.

Step 4: Set a Backup Lock

Like fingerprint recognition, you'll be asked to set a backup method such as a PIN or password for additional security.

Step 5: Complete the Setup

Once the process is complete, you'll be able to unlock your Galaxy S25 just by looking at it, and you can use facial recognition for other functions, such as securing apps or making payments.

Both fingerprint and face recognition are highly effective ways to secure your Galaxy S25, allowing you to unlock your phone quickly while keeping your data safe.

Adjusting Volume and Display Settings

Your Samsung Galaxy S25 comes with a range of customization options to adjust the sound and display settings. Adjusting these settings according to your preference can make your phone experience more enjoyable and tailored to your needs.

Adjusting Volume

Step 1: Open the Settings App

Begin by opening the Settings app on your phone.

Step 2: Tap on Sounds and Vibration

Once you're in the Settings menu, scroll down and tap on "Sounds and Vibration." This is where you can adjust the volume for different sounds on your phone, such as ringtones, notifications, and media playback.

Step 3: Adjust Volume Levels

Under "Sounds and Vibration," you will see individual volume sliders for:

- Media volume: Adjusts the volume of music, videos, and other media content.
- Ring volume: Adjusts the volume of incoming calls and alerts.
- Notification volume: Controls the volume of notifications, such as text messages, emails, and app alerts.
- System volume: Controls the sound of system alerts and notifications.

Simply drag the sliders to the left or right to increase or decrease the volume for each category.

Step 4: Enable Do Not Disturb

If you need to silence your phone temporarily, you can activate the "Do Not Disturb" mode. This will mute notifications and calls without affecting your alarm. You can set specific exceptions for important calls or messages in the "Do Not Disturb" settings.

Display Settings

Step 1: Open the Settings App

To adjust the display settings on your Galaxy S25, go to the Settings app.

Step 2: Tap Display

Once in Settings, tap "Display" to access the screen customization options.

Step 3: Adjust Brightness

In the "Display" menu, you'll see a slider for brightness. Drag the slider to the right to make the screen brighter or to the left to dim it. You can also enable "Adaptive brightness," which automatically adjusts the screen brightness based on your environment.

Step 4: Change Screen Resolution

If you want to save battery life, you can lower the screen resolution. Under "Display," tap "Screen resolution," and you can choose between different levels of resolution: FHD+ (Full HD) for better battery efficiency or WQHD+ for a higher quality display.

Step 5: Enable Night Mode

Night mode reduces the amount of blue light emitted by your phone, making it easier on the eyes in low-light conditions. To enable night mode, go to "Display," and then toggle on the "Dark mode" option. This feature not only helps with eye comfort but can also save battery life on AMOLED screens.

Step 6: Screen Timeout and Always On Display

You can also adjust how long the screen stays on before it turns off. Tap "Screen timeout" and choose a time limit, such as 15 seconds, 30 seconds, or 1 minute. Additionally, the "Always On Display" feature lets you see the time, notifications, and other useful information even when the screen is off.

By adjusting the volume and display settings, you can ensure that your Galaxy S25 fits your preferences, whether you prefer a loud, bright experience or a more subdued, energy-efficient one.

Setting up basic features such as connecting to Wi-Fi, enabling biometric security, and customizing volume and display settings is essential to getting the most out of your Galaxy S25. These settings not only ensure that your phone is secure and connected but also allow you to personalize your device to suit your lifestyle.

Chapter 4: Using the Camera

The Samsung Galaxy S25 has an impressive camera system that allows you to capture high-quality photos and videos. Whether you're taking pictures of your family, friends, or landscapes, the camera provides multiple features and settings to help you get the best shot. In this guide, we will walk you through how to use the camera for photos and videos, explore camera modes like Night, Portrait, and Zoom, and show you how to edit and share your photos.

How to Take Photos and Videos

Taking photos and videos with your Galaxy S25 is easy, and the camera app is designed to be simple to use. Here's a step-by-step guide on how to capture photos and videos:

Step 1: Open the Camera App

To start using the camera, you'll first need to open the Camera app. You can open it by tapping the camera icon on your home screen or from the App Drawer. You can also quickly access the camera by double-pressing the power button on the side of your phone, even if your screen is locked.

Step 2: Switch Between Photo and Video Mode

When you open the camera, you will see several options at the bottom of the screen, such as "Photo," "Video," and other camera modes. By default, the camera will open in "Photo" mode. To switch to video, tap the "Video" option. The camera will start recording as soon as you press the red record button.

Step 3: Taking Photos

To take a photo, all you need to do is tap the white circular button at the bottom of the screen. Make sure to hold your phone steady to avoid blurry photos. You can zoom in or out by sliding your finger up or down on the screen, or by using the volume buttons. If you're trying to capture a fast-moving object or scene, you can use the burst mode by pressing and holding the capture button to take multiple shots in quick succession.

Step 4: Taking Videos

To record a video, switch to "Video" mode by tapping the option at the bottom of the screen. Tap the red record button to start recording, and tap it again to stop. You can also zoom in or out while recording by sliding your finger up and down on the screen.

Step 5: Using the Front Camera

If you want to take a selfie or use the front camera, simply tap the camera switch icon located at the top-right corner of the screen. This will switch from the rear camera to the front camera. Once switched, you can take photos or videos just like you would with the rear camera.

Step 6: Review Your Photos and Videos

Once you've taken a photo or video, a preview will appear in the bottom left corner of the screen. Tap on the preview to open your photo or video. From there, you can edit it, share it, or delete it.

Using Camera Modes (Night, Portrait, Zoom)

The Samsung Galaxy S25 camera comes with a variety of modes to help you capture different types of photos. Some of these modes are designed for specific lighting conditions or photo styles, giving you more control over how your photos look.

Night Mode

Night Mode is perfect for capturing clear, detailed photos in low-light situations, like when you're outside at night or in dimly lit rooms. The camera will use longer exposure times and advanced software to brighten up your photos and reduce noise.

How to Use Night Mode

To use Night Mode, open the Camera app and swipe through the modes at the bottom of the screen. Select

"Night" mode. Make sure to hold your phone steady while taking the photo, as Night Mode requires a longer exposure. Your phone may take a second or two to process the image, but it will help capture more light, resulting in brighter and clearer images.

Portrait Mode

Portrait Mode is ideal for taking photos of people, as it creates a beautiful background blur, making your subject stand out. It uses a special feature called "bokeh" to blur the background, which is great for creating professional-looking portraits.

How to Use Portrait Mode

To use Portrait Mode, open the Camera app and swipe through the modes at the bottom. Tap "Portrait," and then point the camera at your subject. The camera will automatically blur the background, but you can adjust the level of blur by tapping on the "Blur" option on the screen. Make sure the subject is well-lit and within the focus area for the best results.

Zoom Mode

The Galaxy S25 features a powerful zoom function that allows you to get closer to distant objects without losing quality. You can use both optical zoom (which uses the lens) and digital zoom (which enlarges the image using software).

How to Use Zoom Mode

To zoom in or out, simply slide your finger up or down on the screen. You'll notice a zoom slider appear on the screen. You can zoom in up to 10x using the optical zoom, and even more with digital zoom. Keep in mind that the quality of the photo may decrease as you zoom in too much, especially with digital zoom.

Editing and Sharing Photos

Once you've taken your photos, you may want to make some edits to enhance them before sharing. The Galaxy S25 comes with built-in editing tools that are easy to use and allow you to make basic adjustments to your images.

Editing Photos

Step 1: Open the Photo

After taking a photo, tap on the preview in the bottom-left corner to open the image in the gallery. Once the photo is open, tap the pencil icon at the bottom of the screen to enter the editing menu.

Step 2: Crop and Rotate

In the editing menu, you will see options to crop and rotate your photo. To crop, simply drag the corners of the photo to adjust the size. If you need to rotate the image, tap the rotate icon to turn the photo to the desired angle.

Step 3: Adjust Brightness and Contrast

You can adjust the brightness, contrast, and saturation of your photo to make it look better. Tap the "Adjust" option, and slide the bars to adjust the lighting and colors to your liking.

Step 4: Apply Filters

If you want to give your photo a unique look, you can apply filters. In the editing menu, tap the filter icon to choose from a variety of filters. Filters can help make your photos look warmer, cooler, or give them a vintage effect.

Step 5: Add Text or Stickers

If you want to personalize your photo, you can add text or stickers. Tap the text icon to add a caption, or tap the sticker icon to place fun stickers on your photo. You can resize and move these elements around to fit your image.

Step 6: Save Your Edits

Once you're happy with your edits, tap "Save" to keep the changes. You can always go back and make more adjustments later if needed.

Sharing Photos

Once you've edited your photo, it's time to share it with others. The Galaxy S25 makes it easy to share photos via social media, messaging apps, or email.

Step 1: Open the Photo

Open the photo you want to share from your gallery.

Step 2: Tap the Share Icon

In the bottom-left corner of the screen, you'll see a share icon (a circle with three dots connected by lines). Tap on it to open the sharing options.

Step 3: Select a Sharing Method

From the sharing menu, you can choose where you want to send the photo. You can share it via messaging apps like WhatsApp, social media platforms like Instagram or Facebook, or send it by email.

Step 4: Send the Photo

After selecting the app or platform you want to use, follow the prompts to send the photo. If you're sharing on social media, you can also add a caption or tag people before posting.

The camera on your Samsung Galaxy S25 is powerful and versatile, offering a range of features that make it easy to capture great photos and videos. Whether you're taking simple snapshots, experimenting with Night Mode or Portrait Mode, or using the zoom to get closer to your subject, the camera has something for everyone. Plus, with built-in editing tools, you can tweak your photos and share them with others in just a few taps. By mastering these features, you'll be able to take full advantage of your Galaxy S25's camera and create stunning memories.

Chapter 5: Making Calls and Sending Messages

The Samsung Galaxy S25 offers easy-to-use features for making calls and sending messages. Whether you're calling a friend, family member, or colleague, or texting someone, this phone provides all the tools you'll need to stay connected. In this guide, we'll walk you through how to make calls, add contacts, and send text messages. We will also cover how to use WhatsApp, a popular messaging app, to stay in touch with others.

Making Calls and Adding Contacts

Making a call with your Samsung Galaxy S25 is simple and can be done in a few easy steps. Let's break it down:

Step 1: Open the Phone App

To make a call, you need to open the Phone app. You can find the phone icon on your home screen or in the App Drawer. Tap the icon to open the app.

Step 2: Dial a Number

Once the Phone app is open, you will see a dial pad. This is where you can enter the phone number you want to call. Tap the numbers on the screen to dial the phone number. After entering the number, tap the green call button to start the call.

If you're calling someone you've dialed before or saved as a contact, you can also access their number from the "Recents" tab, which shows your recent calls, or the "Contacts" tab, which shows all your saved contacts.

Step 3: Making a Call from Contacts

If you have saved the person's phone number in your contacts, you can find them easily. Go to the "Contacts" tab in the Phone app, and scroll through the list to find the person you want to call. You can also use the search bar at the top to type in the person's name. Once you find their contact, simply tap on their name and then tap the phone icon next to the number to make the call.

Step 4: Using the Favorites Tab

If there are contacts you call often, you can add them to the "Favorites" tab. This allows you to quickly find your most-used contacts. To do this, tap the star icon next to a contact in your list to mark them as a favorite. They will appear in the Favorites tab at the top of your contact list, making it easy to call them.

Step 5: Ending the Call

Once your conversation is over, tap the red "End Call" button to hang up the phone. This will end the call, and you'll be returned to the main Phone app screen.

Adding a Contact

If you want to save a phone number to your contacts for future calls, follow these simple steps:

1. After dialing the number, tap the contact icon (it looks like a little person).
2. A screen will pop up asking if you want to save the number to your contacts.

3. Enter the person's name and any other details, like their email address, and choose a contact group if necessary.

4. Tap "Save" to add them to your contact list.

This way, you'll never have to remember phone numbers again—just open your Contacts and find them quickly.

Sending Text Messages and Using WhatsApp

Sending text messages on your Samsung Galaxy S25 is easy and can be done in the default messaging app or using WhatsApp, a popular messaging app. Here's how to send texts and use WhatsApp:

Sending Text Messages

Step 1: Open the Messages App

To send a text message, open the "Messages" app on your phone. This is where you can view your conversations, create new messages, and send SMS (text) messages to others.

Step 2: Start a New Message

To start a new text message, tap the "+" button or the "New Message" icon, which is usually located at the bottom-right corner of the screen. A new screen will appear where you can enter the recipient's phone number.

Step 3: Enter the Recipient's Number

You can type in the person's phone number manually, or you can tap the "Contacts" icon to select a contact from your saved list. Once you've selected the contact, their phone number will appear in the recipient field.

Step 4: Type Your Message

After you've entered the recipient's phone number, tap the text field at the bottom of the screen to start typing your message. You can type anything you want to say. The keyboard will pop up on your screen, allowing you to type words, numbers, and even emojis. You can also use voice typing by tapping the microphone icon on the keyboard.

Step 5: Send the Message

Once you've written your message, tap the send button (usually a blue icon with an arrow) to send the text. Your message will be delivered to the recipient, and you'll see it appear in your conversation list.

Step 6: Replying to a Message

To reply to a text message, tap on the conversation from the main Messages app screen. Then, type your reply in the text field and tap the send button to send it.

Step 7: Deleting or Archiving Messages

If you want to delete a message, open the conversation, tap and hold the message you want to delete, and choose "Delete" from the options. You can also archive messages to keep them for future reference but remove them from the main screen.

Using WhatsApp

WhatsApp is a messaging app that allows you to send text messages, voice messages, make voice and video calls, and share media like photos and videos. Here's how to use WhatsApp on your Galaxy S25:

Step 1: Download WhatsApp

If you haven't already installed WhatsApp, you can download it from the Google Play Store. Simply search for "WhatsApp," tap on it, and hit "Install" to download it onto your phone.

Step 2: Set Up WhatsApp

After installing WhatsApp, open the app. The first time you use it, you'll need to set it up by entering your phone number. WhatsApp will send you a verification code via text message to confirm your number. Enter the code, and your WhatsApp account will be activated.

Step 3: Add Contacts to WhatsApp

WhatsApp automatically adds people from your phone's Contacts who also use WhatsApp. If you want to message someone, just tap the chat icon in the bottom-right corner of the screen and search for their name. If they're not listed, you can invite them to join WhatsApp by selecting "Invite to WhatsApp" from the app.

Step 4: Sending a WhatsApp Message

To send a message on WhatsApp, tap on the person's name from the contacts list. Then, type your message in the text field at the bottom. You can also send photos, videos, and voice messages by tapping the icons next to the text field. When you're ready to send the message, tap the send button.

Step 5: Voice and Video Calls on WhatsApp

WhatsApp also allows you to make voice and video calls. To start a voice call, tap the phone icon at the top of the chat screen. For a video call, tap the camera icon. The person you're calling will receive a notification, and when they pick up, you'll be able to chat face-to-face.

Step 6: Group Chats on WhatsApp

WhatsApp allows you to create group chats where you can communicate with multiple people at once. To create a group, tap the "New Group" option, select contacts from your phone, and give your group a name. You can then send messages to the entire group, making it easy to communicate with friends, family, or colleagues.

Step 7: Media Sharing on WhatsApp

One of the most popular features of WhatsApp is media sharing. You can send images, videos, documents, and even location details through the app. To share media, tap the attachment icon (the paperclip) in a chat, select what you want to send, and tap "Send."

Making calls and sending messages on your Samsung Galaxy S25 is simple, whether you're using the default Phone and Messages apps or using WhatsApp for more advanced messaging features. The process of making calls and sending text messages is intuitive and straightforward, allowing you to stay connected with others easily. WhatsApp adds extra features like voice and video calls, group chats, and media sharing, making it a powerful tool for communication. By following these easy steps, you'll be able to use your Galaxy S25 to its full potential for calls and messages.

Chapter 6: Exploring Apps and Features

Your Samsung Galaxy S25 comes with a wide range of apps and features that help make your life easier. Whether you want to stay organized, track your health, or make payments with ease, your phone has tools for everything. In this section, we'll explore how to download and organize apps, how to use some of Samsung's special features like Samsung Pay and Samsung Health, and how to set up your email and calendar. Let's dive into these essential features and get the most out of your new phone!

Downloading and Organizing Apps

Step 1: Downloading Apps from the Google Play Store

One of the first things you'll likely want to do with your Samsung Galaxy S25 is download apps. Apps allow you to customize your phone and do everything from checking social media to learning new skills. To download apps:

- Open the Google Play Store app. It's the app with a colorful triangle icon and is typically found on your home screen or in the App Drawer.
- Once inside the Play Store, tap the search bar at the top of the screen and type in the name of the app you want to download.
- Find the app in the search results and tap on it. On the app's page, tap the Install button to begin downloading the app.
- After the app finishes downloading, you can open it immediately by tapping Open or find it in your App Drawer or on your Home Screen.

Step 2: Organizing Apps on Your Phone

As you download more apps, your home screen can start to feel crowded. Luckily, you can organize apps to make your phone easier to navigate. Here's how to organize your apps:

1. Move Apps to Different Pages

To move an app, tap and hold its icon on your Home Screen until it pops up with options. Drag it to a new spot on your screen or to another page by sliding it to the edge of your screen.

2. Create Folders

If you have lots of apps from the same category (e.g., social media, games, productivity), you can group them into folders. To do this, tap and hold one app until it starts to float, and then drag it over another app you want to group it with. When the two apps overlap, a folder will be created. You can name the folder (like "Games" or "Social") and add more apps to it by dragging them in.

3. Remove Apps

If you no longer need an app, you can easily remove it by tapping and holding the app icon, then selecting Uninstall. This frees up space on your phone.

Step 3: Managing App Permissions and Settings

Once your apps are organized, you might want to adjust the settings or permissions of some apps. Go to Settings > Apps to view and manage your apps. Here, you can check which apps have permission to access your camera, location, and more, and you can adjust these settings to protect your privacy.

Using Samsung Features (Samsung Pay, Samsung Health)

Samsung offers its own special apps that bring unique features to your phone. Let's take a look at two of these features: Samsung Pay and Samsung Health.

Samsung Pay: Making Payments Easy

Samsung Pay allows you to make secure payments with your phone, just like you would with a debit or credit card. To use Samsung Pay:

1. Set Up Samsung Pay

First, open the Samsung Pay app on your phone. If you haven't installed it yet, you can download it from the

Google Play Store. Once you open it, follow the on-screen instructions to add your credit or debit cards. You'll need to verify your identity by entering a PIN or using biometric authentication (fingerprint or face recognition).

2. Making Payments

Once your cards are set up, you can use Samsung Pay at any store that accepts contactless payments. To pay, unlock your phone and open the Samsung Pay app. Hold your phone near the payment terminal, and the payment will be processed securely. It's that simple! Samsung Pay also supports loyalty cards, so you can store rewards cards and use them while shopping.

3. Safety and Security

Samsung Pay uses **Samsung Knox** to protect your payment information, so you can shop with confidence. It's safe, easy to use, and accepted at millions of locations around the world.

Samsung Health: Tracking Your Health and Fitness

Samsung Health is an excellent tool for monitoring your fitness and health. Whether you want to track your workouts, steps, or sleep, Samsung Health helps you stay on top of your health goals. Here's how to get started:

1. Setting Up Samsung Health

First, open the Samsung Health app, which comes pre-installed on your phone. If it's not already installed, you can download it from the Google Play Store. Once open, you'll be asked to enter some basic information about yourself, like your age, height, and weight. This helps the app calculate your daily activity and health goals.

2. Tracking Your Activity

Samsung Health lets you track various types of activities, including walking, running, cycling, and even yoga. You can start an activity by tapping on the Exercise tab and selecting the activity you want to track.

The app will record your time, distance, calories burned, and heart rate (if you're using a compatible device like a Samsung smartwatch or fitness band).

3. Tracking Sleep

Samsung Health also tracks your sleep. It gives you insights into your sleep patterns, helping you understand how much time you spend in light, deep, and REM sleep. If you use a Samsung Galaxy Watch or other compatible device, you can get even more detailed sleep tracking.

4. Setting Goals

Samsung Health allows you to set health goals, like walking a certain number of steps each day or exercising for a set amount of time each week. The app will help you stay motivated by showing your progress and offering suggestions for improvement.

5. Connect with Friends

You can also use Samsung Health to connect with friends who use the app. You can challenge each other to achieve fitness goals, which makes staying healthy fun and motivating.

Setting Up Email and Calendar

Step 1: Setting Up Your Email

The Samsung Galaxy S25 comes with an email app that supports multiple email accounts, so you can manage all your emails in one place. To set up your email:

- Open the Email app, which is usually found on your Home Screen or in the App Drawer.
- If this is your first time using the app, you'll be prompted to add an email account. Choose the type of email service you use (Gmail, Outlook, Yahoo, etc.), and enter your email address and password.
- The app will sync your emails, and you'll be able to start sending and receiving messages right away.

Step 2: Organizing Emails

Once your email account is set up, you can organize your inbox by creating folders, labeling messages, or flagging important emails. Simply tap and hold an email to mark it as read, delete it, or move it to a folder. You can also search for specific emails using the search bar at the top of the screen.

Step 3: Setting Up Email Notifications

To make sure you don't miss important emails, you can customize notifications in the *Settings app. Go to Settings > Apps > Email > Notifications* to choose how you want to be alerted when new emails arrive.

Step 4: Setting Up Calendar

The Calendar app on your Samsung Galaxy S25 helps you stay organized by tracking your events, appointments, and important dates. To set up your calendar:

- Open the Calendar app. You can find it on your Home Screen or in the App Drawer.

- To add an event, tap the plus (+) icon at the bottom of the screen. Enter the details of your event, including the date, time, and any reminders you need.
- You can also sync your Google Calendar or other accounts with the Calendar app so that all your events are in one place.

Step 5: Setting Reminders

You can set reminders for your events or tasks to ensure you don't forget anything important. When creating an event, look for the reminder option and select when you want to be notified. You can choose from a variety of options, such as "15 minutes before" or "1 day before."

The Samsung Galaxy S25 is packed with features that make your life easier and more organized. From downloading and organizing apps to using special Samsung features like Samsung Pay and Samsung Health, you can customize your phone to suit your needs. Additionally, setting up your email and calendar ensures that you stay on top of work and personal commitments. By following these steps, you'll be able to make the most of your Samsung Galaxy S25 and enjoy all its powerful features.

Chapter 7: Battery and Charging

The battery life of your Samsung Galaxy S25 plays a crucial role in how well you can use your phone throughout the day. To get the best experience, it's important to understand how to charge your phone properly, save battery power when needed, and even take advantage of wireless charging. This section will explain everything you need to know about charging your phone, saving battery, and using wireless charging.

Charging Your Phone

Charging your Samsung Galaxy S25 is straightforward, but knowing the best practices can help you preserve battery health and keep your phone running smoothly.

Step 1: Using the Correct Charger

When it's time to charge your phone, it's best to use the charger that came with your phone. The Samsung

Galaxy S25 typically comes with a fast charger in the box, so using that charger ensures you get the best charging speed. If you need a replacement charger, make sure to choose a charger with the correct output (usually 25W or higher) for fast charging.

Step 2: Plugging in the Charger

To start charging, plug the USB-C cable into your phone's charging port. The USB-C port is located at the bottom of your phone, and it's used for charging, data transfer, and connecting accessories. Once the cable is securely plugged in, connect the other end of the cable to the power brick (the adapter) and plug it into a wall socket.

You'll know your phone is charging because you'll see a charging icon (a battery with a lightning bolt) at the top of the screen. Additionally, you might notice that your phone will show the charging percentage so you can track how much charge is left.

Step 3: Charging Speed

Samsung's Galaxy S25 supports fast charging technology, meaning it can charge quickly. This means it's best to leave your phone plugged in for 30 minutes or so to give it a quick boost when needed. You'll see a message on the screen that indicates fast charging when it's in progress. If you need a full charge, you may need to leave your phone plugged in for 1-2 hours.

It's also good to avoid using your phone heavily while charging as this could slow down the charging process. If you're in a rush and need a quick charge, try not to use demanding apps like games or video streaming during this time.

Step 4: Charging Safety Tips

While charging your Samsung Galaxy S25, always use quality, certified chargers and cables to avoid any risk of overheating or electrical damage. Make sure to unplug the charger once your phone reaches 100%, as leaving it plugged in too long can affect battery health over time. Most modern phones, including the S25, have built-in safeguards to prevent overcharging, but it's still good practice to unplug when fully charged.

Battery Saving Tips

Sometimes, you may notice that your phone's battery drains faster than you'd like. Whether you're traveling or simply want to make your phone last longer during the day, here are some tips to save battery life on your Samsung Galaxy S25.

1. Reduce Screen Brightness

One of the biggest battery drainers is the screen. To save battery, reduce the brightness of your phone screen. You can do this by swiping down from the top of the screen to open the Quick Settings panel and using the brightness slider to adjust it. You can also enable Adaptive Brightness, which automatically adjusts the brightness based on your surroundings and activity. This feature can help you save battery by dimming the screen when it's not needed.

2. Turn Off Background Apps

Many apps run in the background, using up battery power even when you're not actively using them. To check which apps are consuming battery:

- Go to Settings > Battery and device care > Battery > Battery usage.
- You'll see a list of apps that are using battery in the background. Tap on any app you don't need and choose to Force Stop it.

By turning off apps that aren't in use, you can extend your phone's battery life.

3. Use Power Saving Mode

Samsung Galaxy S25 offers **Power Saving Mode** to help conserve battery life. When enabled, this feature reduces the phone's performance and limits background activity. To enable this mode:

- Open Settings > Battery and device care > Battery > Power saving mode.

2. Toggle the switch to turn on Power Saving Mode. You can also adjust settings within this mode to limit performance, background data, and notifications.

For more control, you can also activate Medium Power Saving or Maximum Power Saving modes for even longer battery life. These modes can limit phone functions like background apps, screen brightness, and more.

4. Turn Off Unnecessary Features

Certain features like Bluetooth, location services, and Wi-Fi scanning can drain your battery when not in use. To save power:

- Turn off Bluetooth when you're not connected to a device (like wireless earbuds or a speaker).
- Disable Location Services by going to Settings > Location and switching it off, or use it only when needed.

- Turn off Wi-Fi scanning (Settings > Location > Wi-Fi scanning), which continuously looks for available networks.

By turning off these features when they aren't necessary, you can save your battery for when you really need it.

5. Limit Notifications and Vibration

Frequent notifications and vibrations can use battery power. You can manage notifications by:

- Going to Settings > Notifications.
- Here, you can choose which apps can send notifications, and you can set them to show silently or with reduced vibration intensity.

By limiting notifications and turning off unnecessary vibrations, your phone can save battery power while still keeping you informed.

Wireless Charging

In addition to traditional charging with a cable, your Samsung Galaxy S25 supports wireless charging, allowing you to charge your phone without plugging in any cables. This can be more convenient and help keep your charging port clean.

Step 1: Setting Up Wireless Charging

To charge your phone wirelessly, you'll need a compatible wireless charging pad or wireless charging stand. Here's how to use it:

1. Place the Phone on the Charging Pad

Simply place your Galaxy S25 in the center of the wireless charging pad. Make sure that the charging pad is plugged into a power outlet and turned on. Your phone should begin charging automatically.

2. Check Charging Status

You'll know that your phone is charging because you'll see a charging icon on the screen. If the charging pad supports fast wireless charging, your phone will display a message indicating fast charging.

Step 2: Wireless Charging Speed

While wireless charging is convenient, it may not charge your phone as quickly as using a wired charger. The charging speed is slower because the power is transferred through the air rather than directly through a cable. However, the Samsung Galaxy S25 supports Fast Wireless Charging 2.0, so you can still charge your phone relatively quickly using the right wireless charger.

Step 3: Using Wireless PowerShare

An exciting feature on your Samsung Galaxy S25 is Wireless PowerShare, which allows you to use your phone's battery to charge other devices wirelessly. You can charge things like wireless earbuds, smartwatches, or even another phone. To use this feature:

- Go to Settings > Battery and device care > Battery.
- Turn on Wireless PowerShare.

- Place the device you want to charge (like wireless earbuds) on the back of your phone.

This feature is especially useful when you're on the go and need to charge another device without needing an additional charging cable.

Step 4: Charging Tips for Wireless Charging

- Place your phone directly in the center of the wireless charging pad to ensure efficient charging.
- Avoid using your phone while it's charging wirelessly, as it may slow down the charging process.
- Keep the charging pad clean and free from dust to maintain efficient charging performance.

Taking care of your phone's battery is essential to ensure you get the best performance from your Samsung Galaxy S25. By following these charging tips, saving battery when necessary, and taking advantage of wireless charging, you can keep your phone running smoothly and efficiently throughout the day. Whether you're charging your phone the traditional way or using the convenience of wireless charging, it's important to practice good charging habits to ensure the longevity of your phone's battery.

Chapter 8: Advanced Features

Your Samsung Galaxy S25 is not just a smartphone; it's packed with advanced features that allow you to do more than you might expect from a typical phone. From transforming your phone into a desktop computer to multitasking with ease, and customizing notifications to suit your needs, this section will cover some of the advanced features that can enhance your experience. These features offer greater flexibility, productivity, and personalization for users who want to maximize their device's potential.

Using Samsung DeX for Desktop Mode

Samsung DeX is a unique feature available on many Samsung devices, including the Galaxy S25. It allows you to transform your smartphone into a desktop computer experience, essentially turning your phone into a mini-PC. With Samsung DeX, you can use your phone like you would a desktop computer, connecting to an external monitor, keyboard, and mouse for a full workstation setup. This feature is ideal for users who want to increase productivity on the go or for anyone who needs to use their phone for tasks usually reserved for a laptop or desktop computer.

How to Use Samsung DeX

To start using Samsung DeX, follow these simple steps:

1. Connect Your Phone to a Monitor or TV

You'll need a compatible USB-C to HDMI cable or a wireless connection to link your Galaxy S25 to a monitor or TV. If using a cable, plug the USB-C end into your phone and the HDMI end into your monitor or TV. For a wireless connection, ensure that both your phone and the monitor/TV are on the same Wi-Fi network and support wireless DeX.

2. Launch DeX Mode

Once connected, your phone will automatically detect the monitor or TV and prompt you to switch to DeX mode. Tap on Start or OK to launch the desktop interface.

3. Using the Desktop Mode

Once you're in DeX mode, you'll see a desktop-like interface on the screen with windows, icons, and a taskbar at the bottom. You can open apps in resizable windows, use a mouse for navigation, and even drag and drop files between apps. The phone screen can function as a secondary display or as a trackpad for easy control.

4. Connecting a Keyboard and Mouse

For the best experience, you can connect a Bluetooth keyboard and Bluetooth mouse to your phone. This will give you full desktop functionality, similar to using a laptop or desktop computer. If you don't have Bluetooth accessories, you can also use a USB keyboard and mouse via a USB-C hub.

Benefits of Using Samsung DeX

Samsung DeX is great for productivity tasks such as word processing, spreadsheet work, web browsing, and even light gaming. It's particularly useful for people who travel frequently and need to access documents, emails, or presentations without the need for a full laptop. Plus, it's an excellent tool for anyone who needs to give presentations using their phone and a projector or monitor.

Multi-Tasking with Split-Screen

The Galaxy S25 is designed to enhance your ability to multitask, and one of the most useful features for this is Split-Screen Mode. This feature allows you to use two apps side by side, so you can get more done without constantly switching between apps. Whether you're texting while browsing the internet, taking notes while watching a video, or using a navigation app while chatting, split-screen is a powerful tool for productivity.

How to Use Split-Screen Mode

To activate and use Split-Screen Mode, follow these steps:

1. Open the First App

Start by opening the first app you want to use. This can be any app, whether it's a messaging app, web browser, or notes application.

2. Activate Split-Screen Mode

Once the first app is open, tap the Recent Apps button (the square icon at the bottom left of the screen). This will show all the apps you have recently used.

3. Select the Second App

In the Recent Apps view, find the second app you want to use. Tap and hold its icon, then drag it to the top or bottom of the screen (depending on your preference) to enable split-screen mode.

4. Adjust the Screen Size

After the two apps are displayed on the screen, you can adjust the size of each app window. Drag the divider between the apps up or down to resize them according to your needs.

Benefits of Multi-Tasking

Split-screen mode is especially useful when you need to interact with two apps at once. For example, you can open a map app while responding to a message, or open a shopping app while reading reviews in a browser. It's a great way to increase your productivity and manage multiple tasks without constantly switching between apps. The Galaxy S25's large, high-resolution screen makes it ideal for split-screen multitasking, providing ample space for two apps to run simultaneously.

Multi-Window Mode

Additionally, you can use Pop-up View for even more flexibility. This allows apps to open in resizable windows that you can move around the screen, giving you even greater control over how you work.

Customizing Notifications

Customizing notifications on your Galaxy S25 can help ensure that you only receive the notifications that matter most. By managing notifications, you can reduce distractions and prioritize the information that's important to you. Samsung provides several options for customizing notifications, from changing notification sounds to adjusting how they appear on your lock screen.

How to Customize Notifications

Follow these simple steps to manage and customize your notifications:

1. Open the Settings Menu

Go to Settings > Notifications to begin customizing how notifications behave on your phone.

2. Choose Notification Categories

Under the Notifications section, you'll see various categories for different types of notifications (e.g., messaging apps, social media, system alerts, etc.). You can choose to enable or disable notifications for individual apps. This allows you to reduce interruptions from apps you don't need notifications from.

3. Customize App-Specific Notifications

If you want more control over a particular app's notifications, tap the app name to open its specific notification settings. Here, you can adjust how notifications appear, change sounds, or disable them entirely. For example, you can decide that you want email alerts to vibrate but not make any sound, while social media notifications can display a visual pop-up alert.

4. Use Do Not Disturb Mode

Sometimes you may need complete peace and quiet, such as during meetings or while sleeping. Samsung offers a Do Not Disturb feature that silences all notifications. To activate it:

● Go to Settings > Notifications > Do not disturb.

- From here, you can set exceptions for certain contacts or apps if you still want to receive important calls or messages while in Do Not Disturb mode.

Additional Notification Customization

Samsung also provides Lock Screen Notifications settings, where you can decide which types of notifications show up on your lock screen. You can hide sensitive content from appearing on your lock screen, or you can choose whether notifications show as icons only or with details.

Notification Sound and Vibration

In addition to adjusting app-specific notifications, you can change the sound for notifications globally. To do this, go to Settings > Sounds and Vibration > Notification Sound. From here, you can select a custom sound, or choose None if you prefer no sound. You can also customize the vibration pattern for notifications, which is helpful if you're in an environment where sound is not ideal.

Importance of Notification Management

Customizing notifications is crucial for managing the constant stream of information your phone receives. By tailoring your notification settings to suit your preferences, you can avoid unnecessary distractions, reduce stress, and focus on the notifications that truly matter. It's especially useful when you need to prioritize important messages or alerts while keeping other, less critical notifications at bay.

Samsung Galaxy S25's advanced features, such as Samsung DeX, multi-tasking with split-screen, and notification customization, significantly enhance the usability of the phone, making it not just a communication device but also a productivity tool. By using these features, you can get more done and personalize your phone to meet your specific needs. Whether you're working on-the-go, managing multiple tasks simultaneously, or fine-tuning how you receive notifications, the Galaxy S25 offers robust options to improve your experience.

Chapter 9: Troubleshooting

Even with a high-tech device like the Samsung Galaxy S25, there may be times when you encounter problems. Don't worry – most issues are simple to fix, and troubleshooting is a straightforward process. In this section, we will cover some of the most common issues that users experience, how to perform a factory reset, and how to update your phone's software to ensure it runs smoothly.

Common Issues and How to Fix Them

Here are some common issues that Samsung Galaxy S25 users might face, along with simple solutions:

1. Battery Draining Quickly

One of the most common complaints about smartphones is the battery running out too quickly. If your Galaxy S25's battery isn't lasting as long as it should, you can try the following:

- Check Battery Usage: Go to Settings > Battery and Device Care > Battery to check which apps are using the most battery. If an app is draining the battery, consider limiting its use or uninstalling it.

- Battery Saver Mode: Turn on Battery Saver mode from the Battery settings to help reduce power consumption. This limits background activity, reduces screen brightness, and disables features like location services.

- Disable Unnecessary Features: Features like Bluetooth, Wi-Fi, or GPS can drain battery life if left on unnecessarily. Turn off these features when not in use by going to the Quick Settings menu.

2. Slow Performance or Lagging

Sometimes, your Galaxy S25 may seem sluggish, and apps might take longer to open. To fix this:

- Clear Cache: Over time, the apps on your phone store data that can slow down the system. Go to Settings > Apps > select the app you want to clear the cache for, then tap Storage > Clear Cache.

- Close Background Apps: Open apps that are running in the background can slow down performance. To close them, tap the Recent Apps button and swipe away the apps you're not using.

- Uninstall Unnecessary Apps: If your phone has too many apps installed, it can slow down. Go to Settings > Apps to uninstall apps you no longer need.

3. Wi-Fi or Bluetooth Connection Issues

If you're having trouble connecting to Wi-Fi or Bluetooth, try the following steps:

- Restart Your Phone: Sometimes, restarting the phone can resolve minor connectivity issues. Simply hold the power button and select Restart.

- Forget and Reconnect: If you're unable to connect to Wi-Fi, go to Settings > Connections > Wi-Fi, tap on the Wi-Fi network you're trying to connect to, and select Forget. Then, reconnect by entering the password again.

- Reset Network Settings: If issues persist, you can reset network settings by going to Settings > General Management > Reset > Reset Network Settings. This will reset Wi-Fi, mobile data, and Bluetooth settings to their default state.

4. Touchscreen Not Responding

If your screen is unresponsive, try these steps:

- Clean the Screen: Sometimes, dirt or moisture on the screen can cause it to be less responsive. Wipe the screen with a soft, dry cloth.

- Restart the Phone: Press and hold the power button to restart your phone, which can often fix a frozen touchscreen.

- Check for Physical Damage: If the screen still isn't working properly, check for any visible cracks or damages. If necessary, take the phone to a service center.

5. Overheating

If your phone feels hot to the touch, it could be due to prolonged use or heavy apps. To cool it down:

- Close Apps: Close apps that are using heavy resources by going to Recent Apps and swiping them away.
- Turn Off Unused Features: Turn off features like Bluetooth, Wi-Fi, or location services if they're not needed.
- Allow the Phone to Cool Down: If your phone is still overheating, turn it off for a few minutes to allow it to cool down.

How to Perform a Factory Reset

A factory reset, also known as a hard reset, will return your Galaxy S25 to its original state when it was first taken out of the box. It's useful if your phone is malfunctioning, running slowly, or you want to erase all personal data before selling or giving it away. Please note that a factory reset will erase all your data, including apps, contacts, photos, and messages, so it's important to back up your data before proceeding.

How to Perform a Factory Reset:

1. Backup Your Data:

Before performing a factory reset, back up your important data. You can do this by going to Settings > Accounts and Backup > Back up data. Choose what you want to back up (photos, contacts, apps, etc.), and follow the instructions to back up your data to Google Drive or Samsung Cloud.

2. Access Reset Settings:

Go to Settings > General Management > Reset.

3. Choose Factory Data Reset:

Under the reset options, tap on Factory Data Reset. You'll be shown a summary of the data that will be erased.

4. Confirm the Reset:

Tap Reset and confirm your choice. You may be asked to enter your PIN or password for security purposes.

5. Wait for the Reset to Complete:

Your phone will restart and begin the reset process. This may take a few minutes. Once completed, your phone will reboot and you will be greeted with the initial setup screen.

Important Note:

After the reset, your phone will be restored to its factory settings, and you will need to set it up again as if it were a new device.

Updating Software

Updating your phone's software is important because it ensures you have the latest features, security patches, and bug fixes. Samsung frequently releases updates to improve performance and address any issues with the device.

How to Update Your Software:

1. Check for Software Updates:

Go to Settings > Software Update > Download and Install. If an update is available, your phone will check for it and begin downloading it automatically.

2. Install the Update:

Once the update has been downloaded, tap **Install** to begin the installation process. Your phone may restart during this process, so make sure you have enough battery life or plug your phone into a charger.

3. Automatic Updates:

You can set your phone to automatically download and install updates when they become available. To do this, go to Settings > Software Update > Auto Download Over Wi-Fi and toggle the switch on.

4. Stay Up-to-Date:

It's important to check for updates regularly to ensure your phone is running the latest software. You can check manually anytime by going to Settings > Software Update > Download and Install.

Why Software Updates Are Important:

Software updates not only fix bugs and issues but also improve security. Without the latest security patches, your phone could be vulnerable to hacking and malware attacks. Therefore, keeping your phone updated is one of the easiest ways to protect your data and ensure your phone operates at its best.

Tips for Updating Your Phone:

- Make sure you're connected to Wi-Fi to avoid using up your mobile data when downloading the update.

- Keep your phone plugged into the charger, especially if the update is large and will take a while to install.

- Be patient: Software updates can take some time, especially if they include major changes or new features.

Troubleshooting common issues, performing a factory reset, and keeping your phone's software up to date are key components of maintaining a smooth, problem-free experience with your Samsung Galaxy S25. By understanding how to resolve typical problems like battery drain, connectivity issues, and slow performance, you can keep your phone running efficiently. In case of more serious problems, a factory reset can return your phone to its original settings, while regular software updates ensure you're always protected and benefiting from the latest features. By following these troubleshooting steps, you'll be able to handle most issues with confidence and ease.

Conclusion

Congratulations on your new Samsung Galaxy S25! With all the powerful features and advanced technology packed into this smartphone, you are bound to enjoy a seamless and efficient experience. Whether you're using it for personal entertainment, professional tasks, or simply staying connected with loved ones, the Galaxy S25 is designed to meet your needs and enhance your daily life.

A Modern Design with Exceptional Performance

From the moment you hold the Galaxy S25 in your hands, you will appreciate its sleek design and premium build. The smooth display, vibrant colors, and impressive screen size make it a joy to use for browsing, watching videos, and gaming. The phone's powerful processor ensures that it runs smoothly, allowing you to switch between apps quickly, stream content without lag, and enjoy a responsive touch interface.

One of the standout features of the Galaxy S25 is its camera system. The ability to take sharp, detailed photos, even in low light, and shoot professional-grade videos gives you the freedom to capture memories in a way that was once only possible with high-end cameras. Whether you're snapping pictures of a stunning landscape or capturing a moment with friends and family, the Galaxy S25 ensures that your photos are crisp and vibrant.

Staying Connected with Ease

The Galaxy S25 offers more than just impressive hardware—it also integrates seamlessly with various software features and applications that keep you connected. Samsung's user-friendly interface, combined with Google's Android operating system, allows you to personalize your device to fit your lifestyle. Whether it's staying in touch with family through messaging apps or managing work emails and calendars, your Galaxy S25 makes these tasks more efficient and easier than ever before.

The integration with Samsung's ecosystem of apps and services, such as Samsung Pay and Samsung Health, allows you to track your fitness goals, make secure payments, and enjoy enhanced digital services right from your phone. With the Galaxy S25, everything you need is at your fingertips, making your life more convenient and productive.

Maximizing Battery Life

One of the most critical aspects of enjoying your smartphone is knowing that the battery will last throughout the day. The Galaxy S25's long-lasting battery, combined with its energy-efficient features, ensures that you can enjoy everything your phone has to offer without worrying about constantly recharging. Whether you're browsing the internet, taking calls, or enjoying media, the Galaxy S25's battery optimizes your usage patterns and provides you with reliable power when you need it most.

Exploring Advanced Features

As you grow more familiar with your new Galaxy S25, you'll begin to explore its advanced features, such as Samsung DeX for desktop mode, multi-tasking with split-screen, and customizing notifications. These powerful tools add a new layer of functionality to your device, enabling you to do more and work smarter.

The Future of Technology at Your Fingertips

Overall, the Galaxy S25 is more than just a phone; it's a tool that empowers you to do more, stay connected, and enjoy entertainment. With its combination of cutting-edge technology, sleek design, and powerful performance, the Galaxy S25 is built for the future, offering you a smartphone experience that is not only satisfying but also inspiring. Embrace all that it offers